Reasons For Renouncing Judaism, And Embracing Christianity: Being An Address To The Children Of The House Of Israel

Henry Samuel Joseph

In the interest of creating a more extensive selection of rare historical book reprints, we have chosen to reproduce this title even though it may possibly have occasional imperfections such as missing and blurred pages, missing text, poor pictures, markings, dark backgrounds and other reproduction issues beyond our control. Because this work is culturally important, we have made it available as a part of our commitment to protecting, preserving and promoting the world's literature. Thank you for your understanding.

REASONS

FOR

RENOUNCING JUDAISM,

AND

𝕰mbracing 𝕮hristianity;

BEING AN ADDRESS TO THE

CHILDREN OF THE HOUSE OF ISRAEL.

BY

HENRY SAMUEL JOSEPH,

FORMERLY READER AND RABBI OF THE SYNAGOGUE AT BEDFORD, NOW TEACHER OF THE HEBREW LANGUAGE.

לְכוּ־שִׁמְעוּ וַאֲסַפְּרָה כָּל־יִרְאֵי אֱלֹהִים אֲשֶׁר עָשָׂה לְנַפְשִׁי׃ *Psal.* lxvi, 16.

"But I will shew thee that which is noted in the Scripture of truth:" *Daniel* x, 21.
"I have found him whom my soul loveth:" *Songs of Solomon*, iii, 4.

NORWICH:
PRINTED BY S. WILKIN, UPPER HAYMARKET;
TO BE HAD ALSO OF MESSRS. BACON AND KINNEBROOK, MATCHETT,
STEVENSON, AND MATCHETT,
PARSONS, STACY, KITTON, MATTACKS, AND JARROLD.

1830.
Price 1s. 6d.

ADVERTISEMENT.

THE author of the following pages submits them to the public with great diffidence, and with a deep consciousness of the imperfect manner in which he has completed the task he assigned to himself. Should any of his readers inquire what induced him thus publicly to make known his reasons for embracing Christianity, his answer is, that, as the *sincerity of his profession* has been called in question by his Jewish brethren, he hopes to show, that, in renouncing the religion in which he was educated, he has been influenced by *a sense of duty*, and not by *worldly motives;* and that the very earnest desire he possesses to address his brethren of the seed of Abraham, on the claims of our Lord Jesus Christ to be received and adored as the promised Messiah, and on the vast importance of a personal and experimental acquaintance with that gospel which he trusts has been the power of God to his own salvation, has been his chief inducement to draw up the following statement. Should this feeble effort of his pen be the means, through the divine blessing, of leading but one of his brethren, according to the flesh, seriously to inquire into the evidences of Christianity and cordially to embrace its truths, he will feel more than rewarded; by such a result he would consider himself highly honoured of the Lord, and abundantly encouraged to persevere through the faith that is in Christ Jesus.

Norwich, No. 97, Pottergate Street, 1829.

REASONS,

&c. &c.

BRETHREN, OF THE HOUSE OF ISRAEL,

ONE of the most eminent of our ancient prophets, the "man after God's own heart," said on a very memorable occasion: "Come and hear, all ye that fear God, and I will declare what he has done for my soul." In similar language I wish to address you, for whom my most unfeigned desire and prayer to God is, that you may be saved. Could you be brought to reflect on the blessedness of heartfelt religion, you would know that a converted Jew cannot but speak to others of the things which he has seen and heard: you would be a witness to what my own experience leads me to affirm, that a true and effectual discovery of Jesus as the Saviour of sinners, to the heart of a self-righteous son of Abraham, must in itself be a sufficient motive to recommend that Saviour to his benighted brethren: for behold the glorious change he experiences; he has been taught from his earliest days to *expect* the Messiah the Son of David, and his daily prayer has been, that "the Redeemer may come to Zion, and to them that turn from transgression in Jacob;" but now, possessed of that spiritual knowledge which results from the spiritual illumination of his mind, he contemplates with astonishment the faithfulness, love, mercy, and glory of God, which so brightly shine in the face of Jesus, in whom he sees fulfilled all the ancient promises in which he trusted; the Messiah whom he expected as a temporal deliverer, he beholds with open eyes, both in his own Scriptures, and in their fulfilment in the New Testament, as the Lamb of God that taketh away the sins of the world, a dying Redeemer, and a life-giving Saviour; a scene infinitely more excellent, infinitely more glorious, than the splendour of a worldly king can display. Such a blessed discovery must be highly calculated to fill the Israelite at once with joy unspeakable and full of glory; with an intrepid zeal to promote the honour of his long rejected Saviour, and with bowels of compassion yearning over his benighted brethren according to the flesh, whom he would fain convince of their darkness and danger, by informing them in what way he has found "Him, of whom Moses and the Prophets did write, Jesus of Nazareth, the son of Joseph," to be the true Messiah.

If this be the state of feeling which a believing reception of Christ as the Saviour of sinners produces, and my own experience in some degree testifies that it is, let it be my apology, if apology be necessary, for the present attempt to address you, however humble my abilities may be. It is not, my dear brethren, from any desire to throw odium either upon your ancient religion, or yourselves, that I now lay before you and the world, my reasons for embracing Christianity; neither does it arise from any desire to flatter or conciliate my Christian friends, or to improve my worldly circumstances; but purely from the humble hope of advancing the glory of God and of my blessed Saviour Jesus Christ, and with a truly sincere desire that you may be induced to examine them minutely and seriously, and that in the perusal you may receive that blessed illumination so necessary to your conversion,—so necessary to your happiness, both in this world and in the world to come, and to the production of that peace of mind which passeth all understanding, which the world can neither give nor take away. Let me then, my brethren, exhort you to enter upon the inquiry, with that candour, sincerity, and seriousness, which its importance demands. Not with the blindness of worldly wisdom, nor the obstinacy of bigotry. Not with a cavilling spirit, but with a broken and contrite heart. Not with a determination of continuing unconvinced, but with the meek and lowly disposition of our blessed Lord and Saviour Jesus Christ—the hope of sinners, the comforter of the afflicted in spirit, and the rock of ages.

If you do this, you cannot fail of arriving at a knowledge of the invaluable truths and comforts of Christianity, those truths that shine like the Sun in the firmament, and which all who seriously and sincerely seek, will surely find; those comforts which drop like the dew from Heaven on the earth beneath, and which are balm to the wounded spirit and the heavy heart.

My reasons for renouncing Judaism and embracing Christianity, may be summed up in the three following particulars:—

First.—Because I found that in Jesus of Nazareth, all the ancient predictions that relate to the Messiah, have received their fulfilment.

Secondly.—Because I found him as the promised Redeemer and Saviour of sinners.

Thirdly.—Because, since by the grace of God, I have experienced what Christianity is, a mighty change has taken place in the feelings of my heart, which I am convinced, with humble confidence, cannot be wrought but by divine power, and is to me a *more* decided evidence than any other, that Christianity is the one only true religion.

1. I found that in Jesus of Nazareth, all the ancient predictions, respecting the Messiah, have received their fulfilment.

It must be allowed, that, as it pleased God to predict the Messiah under certain circumstances peculiar to him, the only way to inquire whether Jesus is that Messiah, as he himself affirmed, is candidly to examine whether these predictions are indeed fulfilled in him. But as all the prophecies cannot be noticed in this short address, the following I trust may suffice. The promise made to our father Abraham, and repeated to Isaac and Jacob,—" And in thy seed shall all the nations of the earth be blessed," Gen. xxvi, 4, —I firmly believe relates to Messiah: that Jesus is the seed proceeding from Abraham is clear, from his well-attested genealogy given in the New Testament, (Matt. 1.); that in him shall all the nations of the earth be blessed, will appear in the sequel, by proving that he is the Saviour of *all* sinners who believe in him; but if the promise relates not to Messiah, I ask, how, then, the nations are or will be blessed in the *seed* of Abraham and Isaac? Our father Jacob foretells that "The sceptre shall not depart from Judah, nor a lawgiver from between his feet, until Shiloh come; and unto him shall the gathering of the people be." לֹא־יָסוּר שֵׁבֶט מִיהוּדָה וּמְחֹקֵק מִבֵּין רַגְלָיו עַד כִּי־יָבֹא שִׁילֹה וְלוֹ יִקְּהַת עַמִּים: Gen. xlix, 10. Jacob is here pointing out to his posterity, the tribe from which, and the time when, Messiah should come. Shiloh is acknowledged by the Jewish writers to be the Messiah. The Targums explain, *until Shiloh come*, by *until the time King Messiah shall come*. It is also allowed by the Targums, the Talmud, and many Jewish commentators, that the word שֵׁבֶט translated *sceptre*, means the royal sceptre of Judah;* but it is manifest that the sceptre *is* departed from Judah, as well as the Lawgiver from between his feet, therefore Messiah is come already.

Daniel, in his famous prophecy of the *seventy weeks*, fixes the coming of Messiah to a certain period, to be calculated from the going forth of *some* decree to restore and to build Jerusalem; and he foretells, that *after* this advent of the Messiah, the sacrifice and oblation shall be caused to cease, that the end of the Jewish nation shall be with a

* The concurrent testimonies of Jewish writers to this truth are to be found in the following: Talmud, Messechet Sanhedrin, Perek א Daff ה and Messechet Harajoth, Perik ג Daff ב in Kimchi, in R. Salomon Jarchi, in Aben Ezra, &c.

flood, or (agreeably to the language of prophecy,) *a hostile invasion*, and that their land shall be laid utterly desolate. Therefore, if the sacrifice and oblation *have been* abolished—if their land has been desolated—then the Messiah *must have* come, because Daniel represents him as coming *before* all these events should take place.

But all these events *have* taken place. More than seventeen centuries have elapsed, since the daily sacrifices in the temple of Jerusalem were abolished; since the Jewish polity was overturned by the hostile invasion of the Romans; and since the whole land of Judæa was desolated by a most destructive war. These circumstances as *matters of fact* cannot be denied. And moreover, Jewish writers themselves, such as R. Solomon, and Jacchiades, own that the sufferings which the Jews experienced at the hands of Titus, were foretold in this very prophecy.

Therefore, since Daniel places the advent of the Messiah *before* the occurrence of these events, and since all these events have *long since* occurred, the Messiah must *long since* have come.

That Jesus of Nazareth is that Messiah, may be collected from the remarkable circumstances, that he is, according to the before mentioned genealogy, of the tribe of Judah; and that, the Sanhedrim and their נָשִׂיא, or *prince*, which was always of the tribe of Judah, retained its power to the latter end of Herod's reign, when Christ was come; and though it was greatly diminished, it had some power remaining, even at the death of Christ; yet quickly after, had none at all: but, my dear brethren, if Jesus be *not* that Messiah, I know not who is; nor can I conceive how any one, who may hereafter claim that office, can prove his descent to be of this tribe, since it is now irrecoverably lost; Israel being scattered among all nations throughout the earth.

We have, further, more than one prophecy that Messiah is to proceed from the loins of David: "And thine house and thy kingdom shall be established for ever before thee: thy throne shall be established for ever:" 2 Sam. vii, 16. "I have made a covenant with my chosen, I have sworn unto David my servant, Thy seed will I establish for ever, and build up thy throne to all generations." כָּרַתִּי בְרִית לִבְחִירִי נִשְׁבַּעְתִּי לְדָוִד עַבְדִּי: עַד־עוֹלָם אָכִין זַרְעֶךָ וּבָנִיתִי לְדֹר־וָדוֹר כִּסְאֲךָ סֶלָה: Psal. lxxxix, 3, 4. "And in that day there shall be a root of Jesse, which shall stand for an ensign of the people; to it shall the Gentiles seek: and his rest shall be glorious:" Isa.

xi, 10: "Moreover I will deliver all the strength of this city, and all the labours thereof, and all the precious things thereof, and all the treasures of the kings of Judah will I give into the hand of their enemies, which shall spoil them, and take them, and carry them to Babylon.—And thou, Pashur, and all that dwell in thine house shall go into captivity: and thou shalt come to Babylon, and there thou shalt die, and shalt be buried there, thou, and all thy friends, to whom thou hast prophesied lies:" Jer. xx, 5, 6. "But thou, Bethlehem Ephratah, though thou be little among the thousands of Judah, yet out of thee shall he come forth unto me that is to be ruler in Israel; whose goings forth have been from of old, from everlasting. Therefore will he give them up, until the time that she which travaileth hath brought forth: then the remnant of his brethren shall return unto the children of Israel."

וְאַתָּה בֵּית־לֶחֶם אֶפְרָתָה צָעִיר לִהְיוֹת בְּאַלְפֵי יְהוּדָה מִמְּךָ לִי יֵצֵא לִהְיוֹת מוֹשֵׁל בְּיִשְׂרָאֵל וּמוֹצָאֹתָיו מִקֶּדֶם מִימֵי עוֹלָם: לָכֵן יִתְּנֵם עַד־עֵת יוֹלֵדָה יָלָדָה וְיֶתֶר אֶחָיו יְשׁוּבוּן עַל־בְּנֵי יִשְׂרָאֵל: Mic. v, 2, 3: which is to this day firmly believed by you; now the same genealogy proves Jesus Christ to be of the extraction of David, and whatever, my brethren, *you* may object to this point, as this short address cannot include many lengthened arguments, I would only remind you that our *fathers*, who lived at the time Jesus was upon earth, though blindly rejecting him, made no such objection; nay, some of them called upon him publicly, "Jesus thou son of David, have mercy upon me;" and when he entered Jerusalem, multitudes received him with, "Hosanna to the Son of David! Blessed *is* he that cometh in the name of the Lord; Hosanna in the Highest!"

The next prediction we shall consider, is a very important one.

"The Lord spake again unto Ahaz, saying, Ask thee a sign of the Lord thy God, ask it in the depth or in the height above." Behold a Virgin shall conceive, and bear a Son, and shall call his name Immanuel: עִמָּנוּ אֵל which you all know signifies, "*God with us*." Isaiah vii, 14. This remarkable prophecy, some have contended, is not to be applied directly to the Messiah; but when we consider the nature of the promise, and how marvellously it was delivered by the mouth of יְהוָֹה himself, we cannot but conclude that something mysterious is included in it, and are persuaded, with some of the Rabbies, that the Messiah is here predicted. The infinite wonder is, that he is *born of a Virgin* and is God *with us*, truly God and truly man; and so in the first chapter of

Matthew, we have an account of the miraculous birth of Jesus, as the direct fulfilment of this. Where, my brethren, is the plausibility of *your* grand objection? "How can Jesus be both God and Man?" Surely it is that marvellous sign which the incomprehensible God, " whose thoughts are not as our thoughts, nor his ways as our ways," condescended to give Ahaz. It becomes us, my brethren, to tremble before we presume to pronounce, and even to cherish an objection against the deep, incomprehensible counsels of the infinitely wise Jehovah; for no other reason, but that the dark, benighted understanding of such poor worms as we are, is unable to account for it.

But this is not the only passage in proof of this blessed truth; the same prophet delineates, in another place, the character of Messiah, in language which made a very striking impression upon my mind, when I first began to inquire after the truth of Christianity: "For unto us a child is born, unto us a son is given: and the government shall be upon his shoulder: and his name shall be called Wonderful, Counsellor, The mighty God, The everlasting Father, The Prince of Peace:" Isaiah. ix, 5. כִּי־יֶלֶד יֻלַּד־לָנוּ בֵּן נִתַּן־לָנוּ וַתְּהִי הַמִּשְׂרָה עַל־שִׁכְמוֹ וַיִּקְרָא שְׁמוֹ פֶּלֶא יוֹעֵץ אֵל גִּבּוֹר אֲבִי־עַד שַׂר־שָׁלוֹם׃ Messiah, the child who is to be born, is (אֵל גִּבּוֹר) "the mighty God,"—the plainest term which the Hebrew tongue can possibly express, a term used in Isaiah x, 21; Jer. xxxii, 18; which all must allow to apply to none but God only: but here is the difficulty you cannot account for—the wonder of "God manifest in the flesh." Let your consciences, my brethren, answer how you can avoid the plain meaning of these texts; as for myself, had I no other proofs from the Old Testament, that Jehovah is to be Messiah, these would satisfy me, for they are the words of the living God, and they cannot be altered: and the Bible is full of this truth. But before I close this part of the subject, I shall bring forward a few passages from our sacred Book to prove to you that Jesus Christ is the same God which created the heavens and the earth, and possesses the divine perfection of Omniscience. I know, my dear brethren, that in your prayers for the day, you repeat *four times:* "Hear, O Israel: The LORD our God is one LORD." שְׁמַע יִשְׂרָאֵל יְהֹוָה אֱלֹהֵינוּ יְהֹוָה ׀ אֶחָד׃ Deut. vi, 4. Now, if Christ be not indeed truly God, then am I, and all Christians who believe that divine worship is to be paid to Christ, guilty of idolatry; for He must either be the God, who made the heavens and the earth, or He cannot be my Lord and Saviour. First, as

Creator:—" Thus saith the Lord, the Holy One of Israel, and his Maker, Ask me of things to come concerning my sons, and concerning the work of my hands command ye me. I have made the earth, and created man upon it: I, *even* my hands, have stretched out the heavens, and all their host have I commanded. For thus saith the LORD that created the heavens; God himself that formed the earth and made it; he hath established it, he created it not in vain, he formed it to be inhabited: I *am* the LORD; and *there is* none else:" Isa. xlv, 11, 12, 18. Now that Christ created the world is evident, from what follows in the same chapter:— " Look unto me, and be ye saved, all the ends of the earth: for I *am* God, and *there is* none else. I have sworn by myself, the word is gone out of my mouth *in* righteousness, and shall not return, That unto me every knee shall bow, every tongue shall swear :" ver. 22, 23: compare these with Phil. ii, 10, 11. And with what majesty does he express himself: " Who hath measured the waters in the hollow of his hand, and meted out heaven with the span, and comprehended the dust of the earth in a measure, and weighed the mountains in scales, and the hills in a balance? All nations before him *are* as nothing; and they are count-

c

ed to him less than nothing, and vanity. Hast thou not known? hast thou not heard, *that* the everlasting God, the LORD, the Creator of the ends of the earth, fainteth not, neither is weary? *there is* no searching of his understanding:" Isa. xl, 12. 17. 28. Now if all this be spoken of God the Father, it argues that Christ is truly God: since it was before shewn that the creation of the world is ascribed to him. But what if all these lofty characters be directly given to Christ? Let every impartial reader judge, when he has maturely considered the context, whether the whole of this fortieth chapter does not correspond with it:—"Comfort ye, comfort ye my people, saith your God. The voice of him that crieth in the wilderness, Prepare ye the way of the LORD, make straight in the desert a highway for our God. And the glory of the LORD shall be revealed, and all flesh shall see *it* together: for the mouth of the LORD hath spoken *it*:" Isa. xl, 1. 3. 5. Compare this with John i, 14: " And the Word was made flesh, and dwelt among us, (and we beheld his glory, the glory as of the only begotten of the Father,) full of grace and truth." Again: "O LORD of hosts, God of Israel, that dwellest *between* the cherubims, thou *art* the God, *even* thou alone, of all the kingdoms of the earth: thou hast made heaven and earth:" Isa. xxxvii, 16. Thus the Psalmist: "For all the Gods of the nations *are* idols: but the LORD made the heavens:" Psal. xcvi, 5. Nay, God himself assures us of the truth of this, when he commands the people of Israel to make it known to the Gentiles: "Thus shall ye say unto them, The gods that have not made the heavens and the earth, *even* they shall perish from the earth, and from under these heavens. He hath made the earth by his power, he hath established the world by his wisdom, and hath stretched out the heavens by his discretion:" Jer. x, 11, 12. So that if Christ were not really God, the Supreme Creator would never allow him to share in this His peculiar honour, by which he distinguishes himself from all creatures. And therefore, since God reveals Christ to us as the Maker of heaven and earth, it is an undeniable proof that He is to be owned by us, as the *true God.*

Secondly. His omniscience! It is asserted by Christ, that "no one knoweth the Father," but the Son; that is, in such a manner as he knoweth him. It is frequently in Scripture asserted, that none but God knows the hearts and thoughts of men: "I the LORD search the heart, I try the reins, even to give every man according to his ways, and according to the fruit of his doings."— אֲנִי יְהֹוָה חֹקֵר לֵב בֹּחֵן כְּלָיוֹת וְלָתֵת לְאִישׁ כִּדְרָכָיו כִּפְרִי מַעֲלָלָיו: Jer. xvii, 10. Yet it is plainly asserted of Christ, that he knows the same: "And needed not that any should testify of man: for he knew what was in man:" John ii, 25. But not only do the apostles speak thus of him, he himself says, "I am he which searcheth the reins and hearts: and I will give unto every one of you according to your works:" Rev. ii, 23. It is no less plain that *almighty power* is ascribed to our blessed Saviour: for he says, in prayer to God the Father, that he had "given him power over all flesh; to give eternal life to as many as he had given him:" John xvii, 2. So he assures his apostles, that all power was given to him both in heaven and in earth: Matt. xxviii, 18. Hence, also, it is apparent that our Saviour Jesus Christ is truly God. But, leaving consequential proofs, let us attend to more express and direct arguments from Scripture. Only one thing may be noticed by the way, as a very considerable argument concerning the divinity of our Lord Jesus Christ; and that is, his being spoken of as Jehovah: for so he emphatically is, by God the Father: "And this is his name whereby he shall be called: *Jehovah our righteousness.*" יְהֹוָה צִדְקֵנוּ: Jer. xxiii, 5, 6. Whether this denotes the very essence of God; or signifies his independency; or his supremacy; or his efficiency; or his eternity; or his immutability; still it is evident that it describes him as necessarily and essentially different from all creatures—". Thus saith the Lord, he that created the heavens:....I have called thee" (that is, Christ, according to the context,) " in righteousness....I am Jehovah; that is my name; and my glory will I not give to another—" אֲנִי יְהוָה הוּא שְׁמִי וּכְבוֹדִי לְאַחֵר לֹא־אֶתֵּן: Isaiah xlii, 8. Since then, he himself gives this name to Christ; and commands us to know and honour him under it; it is a plain demonstration of what that text asserts:—" That all men should honour the Son even as they honour the Father," (John v, 23) being one with himself in essence and dignity. But to proceed to those express passages of Scripture, which speak of Christ as God. I shall refer you only to the apostle's description of him as the God and Sovereign of angels, as well as men: to whom it is commanded they should all worship Him: *vide* Hebr. i, 6, 7. For to which of the angels did God ever say, 'Thou art my son; this day have I begotten thee'? But when he bringeth in the first-born (or first producer of things,) into the world; that is, when he speaks of Christ coming into the world as Mediator, he says, "Let all the angels of God worship him," for by him all things were made, or instituted, and governed before.—Therefore he goes on to show how different Christ and angels are. Of the angels, his ministers or servants, he says that "He made them spirits and a flame of fire. But unto the Son he saith, Thy throne, O God, is for ever and ever. And thou, Lord, in the beginning hast laid the foundation of the earth; and the heavens are the works of thine hands. They shall perish; but thou remainest, &c. To which of the angels said he at any time, Sit thou on my right hand? Are they not all ministering spirits?" So that it is as plain as possible, that Christ is the Head and God of angels as well as of men: and that it is the apostle's object here to prove him to be divine. Now, my brethren, since the apostle brings all his citations from the Old Testament; applying to Christ what is here spoken of the God of Israel; it will hence plainly follow, that He who was then known by the title of God and King of Israel, *was indeed no other than Christ.*

A second reason, which influenced my mind in embracing Christianity, was, that I found Jesus Christ is the promised Redeemer and Saviour.

I am often struck with astonishment at my darkness when a Jew, and at the darkness which alas! still reigns in you, in altogether overlooking that Redeemer which the Lord hath promised to send to Zion, in that passage which I have already quoted; " And the Redeemer shall come to Zion, and unto them that turn from transgression in Jacob, saith the Lord." וּבָא לְצִיּוֹן גּוֹאֵל וּלְשָׁבֵי פֶשַׁע בְּיַעֲקֹב נְאֻם יְהֹוָה: Isa. lix, 20. Of that salvation which is the grand subject of all the prophets,—of that new covenant which the Lord has promised to make in the latter days with his people,—" Behold, the days come, saith the Lord, that I will make a new covenant with the house of Israel, and with the house of Judah: not according to the covenant that I made with their fathers in the day that I took them by the hand to bring them out of the land of Egypt; which my covenant they brake, although I was an husband unto them, saith the Lord: but this shall be the covenant that I will make with the house of Israel: After those days, saith the Lord, I will put my law in their inward parts, and write it in their hearts; and will be their God, and they shall be my people." הִנֵּה יָמִים בָּאִים נְאֻם־יְהֹוָה וְכָרַתִּי אֶת־בֵּית יִשְׂרָאֵל וְאֶת־בֵּית יְהוּדָה בְּרִית חֲדָשָׁה: לֹא כַבְּרִית אֲשֶׁר כָּרַתִּי אֶת־אֲבוֹתָם בְּיוֹם הֶחֱזִיקִי בְיָדָם לְהוֹצִיאָם מֵאֶרֶץ מִצְרָיִם אֲשֶׁר־

הֵמָּה הֵפֵרוּ אֶת־בְּרִיתִי וְאָנֹכִי בָּעַלְתִּי בָם נְאֻם־יְהוָֹה׃ כִּי זֹאת הַבְּרִית אֲשֶׁר אֶכְרֹת אֶת־בֵּית יִשְׂרָאֵל אַחֲרֵי הַיָּמִים הָהֵם נְאֻם־יְהוָֹה נָתַתִּי אֶת־תּוֹרָתִי בְּקִרְבָּם וְעַל־לִבָּם אֶכְתֲּבֶנָּה וְהָיִיתִי לָהֶם לֵאלֹהִים וְהֵמָּה יִהְיוּ־לִי לְעָם׃ Jer. xxxi, 31, 32, 33; of the promised pardon of sins, and upon what grounds we can obtain it,—"Blessed is he whose transgression is forgiven, whose sin is covered. I acknowledged my sin unto thee, and mine iniquity have I not hid. I said, I will confess my transgressions unto the Lord; and thou forgavest the iniquity of my sin." Psa. xxxii, 1, 5. "Thou hast forgiven the iniquity of thy people, thou hast covered all their sin. Thou hast taken away all thy wrath: thou hast turned thyself from the fierceness of thine anger:" lxxxv, 2, 3. For thou, Lord, art good, and ready to forgive; and plenteous in mercy unto all them that call upon thee:" lxxxvi, 5. "Who forgiveth all thine iniquities; who healeth all thy diseases; who redeemeth thy life from destruction; who crowneth thee with lovingkindness and tender mercies:" ciii, 3, 4. "And they shall teach no more every man his neighbour, and every man his brother, saying, Know the Lord: for they shall all know me, from the least of them unto the greatest of them, saith the Lord: for I will forgive their iniquity, and I will remember their sin no more:" Jer.

xxxi, 34. "And I will cleanse them from all their iniquity, whereby they have sinned against me; and I will pardon all their iniquities, whereby they have sinned, and whereby they have transgressed against me:" xxxiii, 8. " In those days and in that time, saith the Lord, the iniquity of Israel shall be sought for, and there shall be none; and the sins of Judah, and they shall not be found: for I will pardon them whom I reserve:" l, 20. "Who is a God like unto thee, that pardoneth iniquity, and passeth by the transgression of the remnant of his heritage? he retaineth not his anger for ever, because he delighteth in mercy:" Micah vii, 18. " To him give all the prophets witness, that through his name (that is the name of Jesus Christ) whosoever believeth in him shall receive remission of sins:" Acts x, 43. " Him hath God exalted with his right hand to be a prince and a Saviour, for to give repentance to Israel, and forgiveness of sins:" v, 31. "And by him all that believe are justified from all things, from which ye could not be justified by the law of Moses:" xiii, 39. "To open their eyes, and to turn them from darkness to light, and from the power of Satan unto God, that they may receive forgiveness of sins, and inheritance among them which are sanctified by faith that is in Christ Jesus:" xxvi, 18.

I say, my brethren, I am struck with astonishment at your entirely overlooking all these gracious blessings, and fixing your hopes upon a temporal deliverer. The cause of this delusion is, that man by nature relishes carnal and temporal, more than spiritual and eternal things; and whilst your minds are taken up with the grandeur of a worldly king, you forget that the above-mentioned spiritual blessings are, according to the Scripture, to be conveyed through the medium of Messiah. That he was to be a Redeemer by being a sacrifice for sin; or in other words one who " saves his people from their sins ;" is established by the passages of scripture we have already quoted, to prove him the Messiah. We have seen that Messiah is called יְהוָֹה צִדְקֵנוּ "Jehovah our righteousness ;" and how? " He takes away our sins, and imparts unto us his unspotted righteousness." We shall now see that "He was wounded for *our* transgressions, and bruised for *our* iniquities." וְהוּא מְחֹלָל מִפְּשָׁעֵינוּ מְדֻכָּא מֵעֲוֹנֹתֵינוּ מוּסַר שְׁלוֹמֵנוּ עָלָיו וּבַחֲבֻרָתוֹ נִרְפָּא־לָנוּ: Isa. liii, 5. " We all like sheep are gone astray," that is, we have departed from God by our sins; but " the Lord hath laid upon *him* the iniquity of us all." כֻּלָנוּ כַּצֹּאן תָּעִינוּ אִישׁ לְדַרְכּוֹ פָּנִינוּ וַיהוָֹה הִפְגִּיעַ בּוֹ אֵת עֲוֹן כֻּלָּנוּ: liii, 6. How? " He was brought as a lamb to the slaughter; he was cut off from the land of the living; he hath poured out his soul unto death." נִגַּשׂ וְהוּא נַעֲנֶה וְלֹא יִפְתַּח־פִּיו כַּשֶּׂה לַטֶּבַח יוּבָל וּכְרָחֵל לִפְנֵי גֹזְזֶיהָ נֶאֱלָמָה וְלֹא יִפְתַּח פִּיו: liii, 7: and for whom? "For the transgression of God's people." "He was cut off, *not for himself*," but for sinners.

If language can at all convey the idea, I see no other conclusion from the passages just quoted, than that Messiah is also the Redeemer and Saviour of Sinners.

Now the new covenant which the Lord hath made with his people, as described by Jeremiah, is, that "he will forgive their iniquities; and remember their sins no more." כִּי אֶסְלַח לַעֲוֺנָם וּלְחַטָּאתָם לֹא אֶזְכָּר־עוֹד: Jer. xxxi, 34. The Messiah therefore is to be a Redeemer, through whom the sins of the people shall be forgiven, and their sins remembered no more; in another place the prophet thus describes the Messiah: "Who is he that cometh from Edom, with dyed garments from Bozrah? I that speak in righteousness, *mighty to save*." מִי־זֶה ׀ בָּא מֵאֱדוֹם חֲמוּץ בְּגָדִים מִבָּצְרָה זֶה הָדוּר בִּלְבוּשׁוֹ צֹעֶה בְּרֹב כֹּחוֹ אֲנִי מְדַבֵּר בִּצְדָקָה רַב לְהוֹשִׁיעַ: וְאַבִּיט וְאֵין עֹזֵר וְאֶשְׁתּוֹמֵם וְאֵין סוֹמֵךְ וַתּוֹשַׁע לִי זְרֹעִי וַחֲמָתִי הִיא סְמָכָתְנִי: Isa. lxiii, 1. 5. "And I looked and there was none to help; and I wondered that there was none to uphold: *therefore mine own arm brought salvation unto me.*" Several Jewish commentators, such as Rabbi Moses Hadarshon, in Berishees Rabba, on Gen. xlix, 2, Perek Eliezer, and Mashmiah Jeshuah agree that Messiah speaks here, and you see he calls himself a *mighty Saviour speaking in righteousness.*

Quotations might be brought forward in great number to prove this point; but I trust these will suffice. Yet I must bring to your recollection what I have attempted to prove in the former part of this address, that Messiah was to be עִמָּנוּ אֵל "God with us;"— אֵל גִּבּוֹר "the mighty God;"—יְהוָה צִדְקֵנוּ "Jehovah our righteousness;" and is it not unnecessary to prove to a Jew, who reads his Bible with any degree of attention, that Jehovah is called the Redeemer and Saviour of sinners? Surely every page of that sacred volume bespeaks its truth. I shall however refer you my brethren to the following passages: "Fear not, I will help thee saith the Lord thy Redeemer." אַל־תִּירְאִי תּוֹלַעַת יַעֲקֹב מְתֵי יִשְׂרָאֵל אֲנִי עֲזַרְתִּיךְ נְאֻם־יְהוָה וְגֹאֲלֵךְ קְדוֹשׁ יִשְׂרָאֵל׃ Isa. xli, 14. "As for our Redeemer, the *Lord of Hosts* is his name." גֹּאֲלֵנוּ יְהוָה צְבָאוֹת שְׁמוֹ קְדוֹשׁ יִשְׂרָאֵל׃ xlvii, 4. "Thus saith the Lord the King of Israel, and his redeemer the Lord of Hosts;" כֹּה־אָמַר יְהֹוָה מֶלֶךְ־יִשְׂרָאֵל וְגֹאֲלוֹ יְהֹוָה צְבָאוֹת׃ Isa. xliv, 6. "Thou shalt know that I the Lord am thy Saviour, and thy Redeemer, the Mighty One of Jacob." וְיָדַעַתְּ כִּי־אֲנִי יְהֹוָה מוֹשִׁיעֵךְ וְגֹאֲלֵךְ אֲבִיר יַעֲקֹב׃ Isa. lx, 16. "Their Redeemer is strong; the Lord of Hosts is his name." גֹּאֲלָם חָזָק יְהֹוָה צְבָאוֹת שְׁמוֹ׃ Jer. l, 34. "Let the words of my mouth and the meditation of my heart, be acceptable in thy sight, *O Lord, my strength and my Redeemer.*" יִהְיוּ לְרָצוֹן אִמְרֵי־פִי וְהֶגְיוֹן לִבִּי לְפָנֶיךָ יְהֹוָה צוּרִי וְגֹאֲלִי׃ Psalm xix, 14.

I now proceed to the third reason, mentioned above, for my profession of Christianity; that since, by the grace of God, I have experienced what Christianity is, a mighty change has taken place in the feelings of my heart.

With shame I must however confess, that when a Jew, the question, "What shall I do to be saved from my sins?" never seriously entered my mind; the reason was, I felt no *need* of a Saviour, my hope was founded upon self-righteousness, and a false notion of the mercy of God.

It was the reading of the New Testament that convinced me not only that I was a

D

guilty, but a helpless sinner. It was in reading that blessed book, that I was brought to see the fallacy of being justified in the sight of a holy and just God, whilst in a state of nature, that is, in a state of sin; and that produced a conviction of the utter impossibility of obtaining acceptance with God without a Mediator; and that Jesus Christ is the only mediator between God and men. I was conscious that the law which God has given us as a rule of our lives, I had often broken, and therefore incurred its *curse;* being further conscious that the commandment must be done with a pure heart, not mingled with sin, since we have to do with a God of purer eyes than to behold iniquity, I was forced to conclude, that no child of Adam can ever keep the law perfectly.

Now, my brethren, the law of God is perfect, converting the soul; and whosoever nameth the name of the Lord, (i. e. with due reverence) must depart from all evil. The same change of heart is necessary both in the Christian and in the Jew, and is set forth at large in the New Testament, especially by Paul in his epistle to the Romans, in which he proves that both Jew and Gentile are under the condemnation of God. In speaking to you, my brethren of the house of Israel, I appeal to the Scriptures of the Old Testament, as affording incontrovertible evidence for the truth of this important fact, and I would also appeal to the conscience of every man, whether he has power to perform, and whether he does actually perform the precepts written in the decalogue—a law equally binding on the Jew and the Gentile, who must both subscribe to the self-evident truth, that its commands are holy, and just, and good, and not to be departed from without just offence to the most high God, who ruleth over all the children of men. We cannot however, it is plain from the express word of God, fulfil this law; for a change must pass upon us, which is the immediate work of God's Holy Spirit, to renew and sanctify our evil hearts, before we are capable of any thing that is good in his sight, or in any wise well pleasing to Him. Remember, my brethren, that it is not our own act: for, say the Scriptures, "Can an Ethiopian change his skin, or a Leopard his spots?" Jer. xiii, 33. Surely it cometh from God.

Now, my dear brethren, I must state to you, that the Jewish religion kept me ignorant of God and myself; nor was it so with me only; alas! truth constrains me to say, it is so with you all. The glory of all God's perfections is the *infinite holiness* of his nature, and to *this*, my brethren, however harsh it may sound to you, if not *professedly*, doubtless *experimentally* you are entire strangers. How did sin, which is so infinitely hateful in the eyes of a holy being, appear in mine eyes? Many indeed are the things upon which I can now look with reverence, which then I slighted, and perhaps scorned; and many that I once beheld with indifference, if not with pleasure, which now I consider as gross and hateful sins. As no knowledge of divine justice can be possessed by any one who cherishes hopes of forgiveness without paying, or one having paid for him, the due punishment for the breach of the holy law, surely as a Jew outwardly I could have no idea of it. Nay, my brethren, truth leads me to conclude, that whosoever looks for the salvation of his sinful soul to any other method than that which God himself has graciously given us; namely, through the promised Redeemer Jesus Christ, does actually rob the Almighty of one of his attributes, *his infinite justice*. Now should you be ready to ask, Where is the mercy of God? I must tell you, that a Jew can have no *real* knowledge of the mercy and love of God, as long as he rejects the Lord Jesus Christ: it is in giving his only-begotten Son to be a sacrifice for us, poor, polluted, sinful, creatures, that the infinite love and mercy of God shine in all their brightness; and to say that the Almighty displays his mercy in pardoning sinners *without an atonement*, is to destroy one of his divine attributes, and to depreciate others, and so to " darken counsel by words without knowledge."

Further, I had, under Judaism, no knowledge of myself. I never could believe that the heart of man is deceitful above all things, and desperately wicked. Jer. xvii. 9. I have in my prayers confessed myself a sinner, while the secret language of my heart was, I am as good, as just, as kind, and as humble, as most of those with whom I associated;—the pride, the deceitfulness, and wickedness of the heart, were so entirely hid from me, that I had scarcely any thought even of repentance.

But, all glory be to God, I humbly trust it is not so with me now. I would, at the same time, have my reader remember, that I presume not to boast of a thorough knowledge of God, or myself; far be such a thought from me: " Who can by searching find out God?" And (as I before quoted the words of the prophet,) " The heart of man is deceitful above all things, and desperately wicked; who can know it?" Nor would I boast of a particular measure of grace;— how can I, in the face of the many infirmi-

D 2

ties which I have reason to bewail? Yet to declare the mercy of the Lord, my conscience testifies that since I have been favoured with a knowledge of the gospel, I have experienced new manifestations of the awful majesty and holiness of God, as well as of the odiousness and misery of sin; and especially the danger to which my sins exposed me; *when I was living neither as a Jew nor a Christian, and blasphemed the name of my blessed Lord and Saviour, Jesus Christ.* I trust the Spirit of the Lord has implanted in my soul some thirst after his righteousness, so that I may say, with humble confidence, "The desire of my heart is to have God, and him only, for my everlasting portion, to love and serve him, and him only." Thanks be to God, I now know enjoyments to which I was before a stranger, and which the world can neither give nor take away; arising from communion with God in public, social and private prayer,—from reading and meditating upon the blessed tidings of the gospel,—from having an opportunity of preaching the blessed Gospel of my Lord and Saviour Jesus Christ,—from conversation with the children of God, (I mean my dear Christian friends and brethren.) My hopes are set upon " an inheritance incorruptible and undefiled, that fadeth not away, reserved in heaven for all those who are the children of God by faith in Jesus Christ."

No, my brethren, it is not my own heart that has at once changed itself; of that I am fully convinced, since I experience still its wickedness and deceitfulness, and I am confident that if we are left but one moment to ourselves, that very moment may prove fatal to all eternity! It is by the grace of God only I can truly say, "I am what I am." My earnest prayer is that I may be kept under the guidance of his holy Spirit; that I may not in any wise degrade my christian calling; but that I may " let my light so shine before men, that they seeing my good works may glorify my Father who is in heaven." I am further convinced, it is not the work of men; for whatever external changes may be effected by human exertions, one thing is *sure*,—no man can work effectually upon the *heart* of another, no human strength can implant new desires and affections.—I know that you will be ready to say it is the work and power of Satan: now we know that the great object that Satan has in view, is to lead us from the way of life, into the broad road of destruction.

What does he desire more than a creature should be indifferent about his eternal condition, and pursue the path of sin? which was exactly my Jewish character. No, the above account of the change I have experienced, which I trust has not been hypocritical, *is not the work of the* adversary of God and man; and since it is neither the work of myself, or any other man, I have the greatest reason possible to conclude it is the working of the Holy Spirit, and the will of God, and his gracious providence, that has led me to this happy way, for it is his own, and that of his chosen servants.

I must say with the psalmist of old, "Bless the Lord, O my soul; and all that is within me, bless his holy name:" Psalm ciii, 1.

I must now state to you how frequently I was struck with this fact, when a Jew outwardly—that when the children of Israel were the chosen people of God, they were obliged to have *both sacrifices and a Mediator; whom have we now? or what have we now for a remission of sins?*

Now you know that the lesson taught you by Moses, is this, that you must be saved altogether by an atoning sacrifice. This is taught you throughout the whole ceremonial law: the daily and annual sacrifices proclaimed it to our whole nation. Nor was this taught merely in theory: it was required of every offender, whatever his sin might be, to bring his sacrifice, in order that it might be put to death in his stead, and deliver him from the condemnation which his sin had merited. Even for sins of ignorance, this was required; and the offender was *to put his hands on the head of his sacrifice*, and thus to transfer to it his sins.

On the great day of annual expiation, (i. e. יוֹם כִּפֻּר) the High Priest, after killing the goat on which the Lord's lot had fallen, was to put his hands on the Scape-goat, and to confess over him, all the sins of all the children of Israel; and then the goat was led into the wilderness, from before them all, never more to be seen: that so the removal of their sins might be made visible, as it were, to their bodily eyes.

Yet whilst this glorious truth was thus plainly discovered, the insufficiency of the legal sacrifices, and the necessity of a better sacrifice was proclaimed also. For these very sacrifices were to be repeated from year to year, which shewed that the guilt expiated by them, was not fully removed.

Hence the very sacrifices were in fact no other than an annual remembrance of sins, not finally forgiven. In this light they were viewed by the apostles of our blessed Lord Jesus Christ. The apostle Paul observes, "For the law having a shadow of good things to come, and not the very image of the things, can never with those sacrifices which they offered year by year continually make the comers thereunto perfect. For then would they not have ceased to be offered? because that the worshippers once purged should have had no more conscience of sins. But in those sacrifices there is a remembrance again made of sins every year." Heb. x, 1—3.

The same thing was intimated by the very partial appointment of sacrifices. There were many sins, as adultery and murder, for which no sacrifices were specified. Nor in truth, was any man made perfect, as pertaining to the conscience by any of his sacrifices, because every man had a secret suspicion at least, if not conviction, that the blood of bulls and goats could never take away sin. Still however the great end was answered, of directing the eyes of all to the appointed sacrifices, and through them to the Lord Jesus Christ, the great sacrifice, whose blood alone can cleanse from sin, and who is "a propitiation for the sins of the whole world."

O my dear brethren, let your eyes be directed to the same sacrifice, even to your Messiah the Lord Jesus Christ. This is he whom our fathers pierced and nailed to the cross: and through whom thousands of those who crucified him, found peace with God: and if you also, could now be persuaded to look unto him for salvation, you would immediately experience the effect produced by the brazen serpent in the wilderness, and be healed every one of you.

Allowing however, the greatest efficacy to those sacrifices which were offered by the law, you now have *not* even them to fly to for refuge: they have long ceased among you, and left you destitute of any certain hope, that God will accept your repentance, and blot out your misdeeds. Your law expressly declares that it is the blood that maketh an atonement for the soul: if then you are without hope in the *blood of Christ*, who was to cause your sacrifices and oblations to cease, where else will you seek for the propitiation of your sins; sins which you cannot but be sensible you have knowingly and repeatedly committed against the positive commands of your God? And does not the remembrance of them sometimes break in upon your peace of mind, and fill you with alarming doubts and perplexities? Are there not some moments, when you wish in your hearts for a stronger assurance of forgiveness than you can possibly derive from your law? And will you not stand in the utmost need of it at your last hour, when you are leaving this world, to appear in the presence of a righteous God, "who will bring every work into judgment, with every secret thing, whether it be good, or whether it be evil?" Eccles. xii, 14.

Know, then, my brethren, that "there is no salvation in any other, neither is there any other name given under heaven, among men, whereby they must be saved, but only the name of *Jesus.*" Acts, iv, 12. "Look therefore unto him, and be ye saved." Isa. xlv, 22. "Be ye not stiff-necked as your Fathers were, but yield yourselves unto him, that you may at length find deliverance from all your afflictions, may be reinstated in the favour of God, may be partakers of the inestimable privileges of the new covenant, and may become part of that "one fold under one Shepherd, Jesus Christ, the righteous." John x, 16. 1 John ii, 1.

Having thus, my dear brethren, endeavoured to lay before you my reasons for embracing christianity, I cannot but tell you that I not only heartily rejoice in what the Lord has done for *me*, and in the "love of Jesus Christ shed abroad in my heart," (Rom. v, 5,) but that it is my sincere desire and fervent prayer to our God, that he may also open *your* eyes, and teach you the "truth as it is in Jesus:" Eph. iv, 21. May I not then entreat you, with brotherly affection, to "search diligently whether these things be so?" Acts. xvii, 11. Search the Scriptures for yourselves: "search them as for hid treasures." Prov. ii, 4, 8. Pray to God to give you his Holy Spirit to instruct you, "and to guide you into all truth:" John xvi, 13. When you take the blessed book of God into your hands, lift up your heart in prayer to him, and say with David, " Open thou mine eyes that I may behold wondrous things out of thy law." גַּל־עֵינַי וְאַבִּיטָה נִפְלָאוֹת מִתּוֹרָתֶךָ: Psalm cxix, 18. Then compare the Old Testament with the New: and mark how exactly they correspond with each other, even as the vessel with the mould, or the wax with the seal.

Then I fear not but that you will soon acknowledge Him of " whom the law and the prophets do speak, even Jesus of Nazareth," (John i, 45,) to be the true Messiah, and the Redeemer and Saviour of Sinners. Yes, he whom you have hitherto rejected, will become precious to your souls; and you will in a far higher sense than you have ever yet been, become the children of Abraham, the Sons of God. Let me again recommend to you the reading of the New Testament, and if you do but read it with a true spirit of enquiry, and not with the feelings of controversy, the Lord will bless the reading of it to your souls, and you will there find that our Lord Jesus spoke to his disciples of the death which he should accomplish at Jerusalem. He taught them "that he must suffer many things, and be rejected of the Elders, and of the Chief Priests and Scribes, and be killed; and after three days rise again," (Mark viii, 31; Luke ix, 22,) in order that the "things might be fulfilled which were written in the Law of Moses and in the Prophets, and in the Psalms, concerning Him." Luke xxiv, 44. He also called them to witness that he would rise from the dead on the third day, as a proof, beyond all doubt, unto them and unto all men, that he was the true Messiah. It belongeth only "to God, to raise the dead:" Acts xxvi, 8. And Jesus was raised from the dead, as he had said, and thus it was proved that he was the Son of God as he had declared. In conclusion, let me intreat you "to suffer the word of exhortation;" Heb. xiii, 22. Let me exhort you to consider, *First*, The importance of a personal consideration of the truths to which I have already referred you. *Secondly*. To seek a real knowledge of God and of yourselves. *Thirdly*. To seek a sacrifice, and also to examine yourselves, and inquire diligently respecting the circumcision of the heart. You will say, perhaps, that in all this, I am bringing, by implication at least, a very heavy charge against you and your nation.

Alas! my brethren, facts compel me to bring this heavy charge, not against you in particular, but *against human nature*, of which both you and I, both Jew and Gentile, are all alike partakers. Let us, therefore, be humbled together; and, if in any thing we have more light and knowledge, or a better spirit than others, let us say, "Not unto us, O Lord, not unto us, but unto thy name give glory, for thy mercy and for thy truth's sake." Psalm cxv, 1. For by nature, we are as others; and therefore it is needful that the word of counsel and exhortation on these important subjects, should be freely given and received in love. We are fellow-travellers to eternity: and when the interests of our immortal souls are concerned, we cannot be too faithful, or too earnest with each other. Accept it, therefore, as the counsel of a brother, that I exhort and intreat you, by all that is awful and precious, in time and eternity, to search and examine your own heart, whether thus far you have not rested too much in the externals and ceremonies of your religion, without duly considering wherein consists its life and power, or earnestly searching the Scriptures, to discover what are its great and essential doctrines, and what is indeed the true and only way of salvation.

I do not desire that you should look to me as a teacher, or take for granted without examination any thing that I say: but earnestly advise you to search into this matter diligently and humbly, as knowing the value of your own immortal soul, and feeling how necessary it is that, *in all that bears reference to eternity, you should go upon sure grounds:* "For what shall it profit a man, if he gain the whole world, and lose his own soul? or what shall a man give in exchange for his soul?" Mark viii, 36. It is written; "The way of a fool is right in his own eyes: but he that hearkeneth to counsel is wise:" Prov. xii, 15. Do not therefore rashly conclude that you are right, but hearken to counsel, and I trust you will one day find reason to rejoice, and to be thankful to him, whose providence has brought this warning into your hands.

First, I will exhort you then, to seek and to maintain clear views of the divine character, as revealed in those Scriptures, which you yourselves acknowledge "to be given by inspiration of God:" 2 Tim. iii, 16. Consider especially with what a *holy* God you have to do;—" For the Lord thy God is a consuming fire, even a jealous God:" Deut. iv, 24. We are apt to overlook this part of the divine character, though it is his great and peculiar glory that He is *holy.* "Who is like unto thee, O Lord, among the Gods? Who is like unto thee, glorious in holiness, fearful in praises, doing wonders?" Exod. xv, 11.

We are disposed to satisfy ourselves with vague ideas of his goodness and mercy,—as if he had scarce any thing to do, but to pardon our offences, as often as we committed them. But "to him belongeth vengeance and recompence; for the Lord will judge his people." Deut. xxxii, 35, 36. Our great concern is with him, as a moral governor and righteous judge. "The Lord is our judge, the Lord is our lawgiver, the Lord is our king." Isaiah xxxiii, 22.

And you should be careful not to forget his peculiar glory and most distinguishing attribute: "God is love." 1 John iv, 8. This is most true: but let us remember that his infinite love of all that is holy and lovely implies a corresponding abhorrence of whatsoever bears a contrary character. There is nothing that our narrow, darkened, and depraved minds are more slow to conceive, than the infinite repugnance and hatred of such a pure and glorious being, to every trace of sin and pollution. Yet the consideration of that spotless purity should influence all our approaches to God; that is to say, every act and sentiment of devotion. Neither can any thing be more important in religion, than just views of the character of him, who is the object of our adoration and love. So important is this, according to the scriptures, that they often put *the knowledge of God* for religion at large, as comprising the sum and substance of it. And in what way religion takes its character from the holiness " of him with whom we have to do," (Heb. iv, 13) we may understand in some measure, from its being so frequently called *The fear of God*. As children of Israel, you have special reason to consider this point. For wherefore are all those judgments and fearful curses poured upon your nation, under which you have been suffering for so many hundred years? "That thou mayest *fear* this glorious and fearful name—The Lord thy God:" Deut. xxviii, 58.

And amidst all the contemplations of his mercy, it must never be forgotten, that "His name is holy," and he is expressly "the Holy One of Israel:" Isa. liv, 5.

" God is greatly to be feared in the assembly of the saints, and to be had in reverence of all them that are about him:" Ps. lxxxix,

"The fear of the Lord is the beginning of wisdom; and the knowledge of the Holy is understanding." Prov. ix, 10. And if we do not rightly fear him, we shall never truly love him.

Secondly. Next to just views of the divine character, it is most needful to have just views of ourselves. For religion becomes unprofitable and impracticable, unless it is adapted to the state and character of the being who is the subject of it.

We find accordingly, that the religion of the scriptures, while it evidently bears, in all its branches, the seal and impress of the holy character of its author, is also most wisely and wonderfully adapted to the case and necessities of a fallen and sinful, and therefore weak and miserable creature, such as man is uniformly represented to be. Understand therefore, and acknowledge *your own sinfulness*. This will naturally follow from clear views of the divine character, and from the contemplation of his holiness and glory. Thus when Isaiah had seen the glory of the Lord, and heard the songs of the angels, crying, "Holy, holy, holy," he was humbled in the dust, under a sense of his own guilt and pollution. "Then said I, woe is me, for I am undone; because I am a man of unclean lips, and I dwell in the midst of a people of unclean lips: for mine eyes have seen the King, the Lord of Hosts:" Isa. vi, 5. And such also was the effect of similar revelations upon holy Job, "I have heard of thee by the hearing of the ear: but now mine eye seeth thee. Wherefore I abhor myself, and repent in dust and ashes:" Job xlii, 5, 6. Seek to have your minds filled with a solemn sense of the presence of that holy, glorious, and heart-searching being, and then consider how great and manifold have been your transgressions against his pure, and good, and perfect law, in thought, word, and deed, from your youth upward even until now.

Do not flatter yourselves that there are such and such crimes, of which no man can accuse you: "for *the Lord* seeth not as man seeth; for man looketh on the outward appearance, but the Lord looketh on the heart." 1 Sam. xvi, 7.

And the same authority which saith "Thou shalt not kill; Thou shalt not commit adultery; Thou shalt not steal; thou shalt not bear false witness;" says also, with equal solemnity, "Thou shalt not *desire* thy neighbour's wife; Thou shalt not *covet* any thing that is his." And who can stand under a commandment which applies to the inmost purposes, and secret wishes of the heart? Think of this, and I may justly ask with

Eliphaz, " Is not thy wickedness great, and thine iniquities infinite?" Job xxii, 5. And, above all, how little have you loved God! how unthankful have you been for his daily and hourly mercies!—though every breath you draw, and every pulse of your heart, brings with it some fresh token of his love and care! How have you forgotten him, hours and days without number, though the whole earth is full of his glory, and manifest footsteps of his wisdom, power, and goodness, offer themselves to view in every creature! Nothing would more impress us with the sense of our own guilt, than to bring our own coldness, forgetfulness, and ingratitude into contrast with the lovingkindness and the glories of the Lord. Do not attempt to deny or conceal your guilt—" do not cover your transgression as Adam, by hiding your iniquity in your bosom;" (Job xxxi, 33;) but rather follow the example of David—" I acknowledge my sin unto thee, and mine iniquity have I not hid. I said, I will confess my transgressions unto the Lord; and thou forgavest the iniquity of my sin:" Ps. xxxii, 5. To make any pretensions to innocency before God, is hateful presumption in his sight: " Thou sayest, Because I am innocent, surely his anger shall turn from me: *Behold, I will plead with thee, because thou sayest, I have not sinned:*" Jer. ii, 35.

To deny our guilt would, indeed, be a direct contradiction of all those plain statements, respecting our moral condition, which we have already quoted, and which are pronounced against us, by his certain and indisputable judgment, who alone "searcheth the heart and trieth the reins, to give every man according to his ways, and according to the fruit of his doings:" Jer. xvii, 10. Those declarations, my brethren, apply distinctly *to you* and *to me*—for they are true of each individual among the children of men.

Let us, therefore, humbly unite in the confession, " We lie down in our shame, and our confusion covereth us ; for we have sinned against the Lord our God, we and our fathers, from our youth even unto this day, and have not obeyed the voice of the Lord our God :" Jer. iii, 25.

Thirdly: Under this deep sense of your own guilt, and unworthiness, and pollution, you must seek acceptance with that holy and glorious God, *in his own appointed way.*

This is a point of momentous importance to every child of Israel. You can no longer offer any sacrifice after the manner of your fathers, or according to your law. Your temple is destroyed, and all its rites and ordinances utterly abolished. You have no longer any High-priest, who on the solemn day of atonement, may enter into the Holy of Holies, to make reconciliation for your sins. To *you*, therefore, the way of access to God is utterly closed, if you look no further than to your own law, and the Scriptures of the Old Testament.

You will say that you now look for acceptance with God, by means of repentance, and that true repentance serves you instead of a sacrifice. But is it not evident, from the foregoing statement of scripture doctrine, that in all such assertions, you are grossly confounding things perfectly distinct?—each absolutely necessary in its own place, but neither availing in the absence of the other.

Repentance is needful—yea indispensable: but the consideration of it belongs to the doctrine of that change of heart, and inward renewal of the mind and spirit, of which I have spoken in the former part of this address, and not to the doctrine of the sacrifice. No sacrifice ever availed to procure any spiritual blessing for the impenitent:—no repentance ever did, or ever will avail without sacrifice. Repentance and a sacrifice were both of them always necessary to the salvation of a sinner,—and they are so still. It is therefore a matter of unspeakable importance, to the peace and welfare of your immortal souls, to inquire, *where is* now your *sacrifice?*

Observe then, I entreat you, that *we* who believe in Christ have a sacrifice, though *you* who despise him have not.

We have one all-sufficient sacrifice, of the value and efficacy of which, not all the powers upon earth can deprive us, unless they could avail to recall the past, and undo the finished work of the most high. *We*, under a sense of all our guilt and unworthiness—and let the number and magnitude of our offences be aggravated to the utmost,—*we* can look to the Lord Jesus Christ and say, " Behold the Lamb of God, that taketh away the sins of the world:" John i, 29. " For by one offering, *he* hath perfected for ever them that are sanctified : whereof the Holy Ghost is a witness unto us:" Heb. x, 14, 15. So that we may humbly yet boldly say, " Who is he that condemneth ? it is Christ that died:" Rom. viii, 34. " We have a strong consolation, who have fled for refuge to lay hold upon the hope set before us; Which hope we have as an anchor of the soul, both sure and stedfast:" Heb. vi, 18, 19. And while for ourselves we rejoice in the fulness and all-sufficiency of this great and only sacrifice, we would earnestly entreat *you* also to become partakers of our joy. Come then to this atoning Lamb, and lay your hand by faith upon his head, and cast all the burthen of your accumulated guilt upon Him, " who was wounded for our transgressions, and bruised for our iniquities: the chastisement of our peace was upon Him, and with his stripes are we healed:" Isa. liii, 5. It is *our* rejoicing,—let it be also yours—" that being justified by faith, we have peace with God, through our Lord Jesus Christ: by whom also we have access by faith into this grace wherein we stand, and rejoice in hope of the glory of God.—For when we were yet without strength, in due time Christ died for the ungodly.—Much more then, being now justified by his blood, we shall be saved from wrath through Him. For if, when we were enemies, we were reconciled to God by the death of his Son, much more, being reconciled, we shall be saved by his life. And not only so, but we also joy in God, through our Lord Jesus Christ, by whom we have now received the atonement:" Rom. v, 1, 2, 6. 9, 10, 11.

This is *our* sacrifice; and you at this time have, and can have none other. If Jesus Christ be not an all-sufficient sacrifice for sin,—and if you do not accept him and trust in him as such,—it is evident that you never can receive any of those benefits which sacrifice was appointed to convey. Or, in other words, you are utterly destitute of any way of access by which you can approach to God with acceptance. "Your iniquities have separated between you and your God, and your sins have hid his face from you:" כִּי אִם־עֲוֹנֹתֵיכֶם הָיוּ מַבְדִּלִים בֵּינֵכֶם לְבֵין אֱלֹהֵיכֶם וְחַטֹּאותֵיכֶם הִסְתִּירוּ פָנִים מִכֶּם מִשְּׁמוֹעַ׃ Isaiah lix, 2. There is a mighty gulf of separation between you and him, which no human power or wisdom can avail to cross. "For He is not a man, as thou art, that thou shouldest answer him, or that you should come together in judgment. Neither is there any days-man betwixt you, that might lay his hand upon you both:" Job ix, 32, 33. Finally, I would urge upon your attention the statements I have quoted from your own Scriptures, respecting an inward change and renewal of the heart. If these be indeed the true sayings of God, it is of unspeakable importance that you should consider them well, and seriously and diligently inquire, whether *you* have experienced this inward and spiritual change, or not?

You are children of Abraham: but have you Abraham's faith? and do you perform the works of Abraham? You are outwardly circumcised: but is your heart circumciseth unto the Lord? Have you cast away all your transgressions, and made you a new heart and a new spirit, according to the word of God, by his prophet Ezekiel. Hath God taken away the stony heart out of *your* flesh, and given *you* a heart of flesh, and put his spirit within *you*, to cause you to walk in his statutes, and to keep his judgments, and do them? Ezek. xxxvi, 26, 27.

These and similar questions you should put very closely to yourselves, as in the sight of the heart-searching God; and you should seriously "consider your ways:" Hag. i, 7.

It is vain, my brethren, to make your boast of Abraham and the prophets, unless you follow the example of their faith and holiness. "God is no respecter of persons:" Deut. x, 17: 2 Chron. xix, 7: Acts x, 34. If our fathers were a highly favoured and peculiar people, the greater was their condemnation for their abuse of their privileges: for thus it is written in one of your own prophets, "You only have I known of all the families of the earth: therefore will I punish *you* for all *your* iniquities:" Amos iii, 2. As if it were said, Other nations are in darkness and ignorance; their privileges and opportunities are few and small. "Little has been given, and therefore little will be required." They will be punished indeed in their measure, for "The wicked shall be turned into hell, with all the nations that forget God."

Psalm ix, 17. But you are highly favoured; you have the Scriptures in your hands, "which are able to make you wise unto salvation:" 2 Tim. iii, 15.—Therefore every iniquity and transgression which you commit has great aggravations, and must be visited accordingly, when "God shall bring every work into judgment, with every secret thing, whether it be good, or whether it be evil." Eccl. xii, 14. According to your peculiar privileges, is your peculiar guilt, if you transgress; and equally memorable must be your heavy condemnation and punishment, when the Lord shall whet his glittering sword, and his hand shall take hold on judgment, and he will render vengeance to his enemies, and will reward them that hate him: Deut. xxxii, 41. That you are the children of Abraham, proves nothing but what you *ought* to be. Korah, Dathan, Abiram, were the children of Abraham as well as you,—and so were all the people of that evil generation, respecting whom "the Lord sware in his wrath that they should not enter into his rest:" Psalm xcv, 11. And so were those whom Jeremiah and Ezekiel so severely rebuked, and who yet remained impenitent under the plainest declarations of God's wrath, and even under the execution of his judgments against them. It is therefore very possible, that, with all your privileges as a chosen and peculiar people, you may yet be altogether *uncircumcised in heart;* (Ezek. xliv, 7; Acts vii, 51;) for such was the case with those who lived in the time of Jeremiah: "Behold the days come, saith the Lord, that I will punish all them which are circumcised and uncircumcised." 'Egypt, and Judah, and Edom, and the children of Ammon, and Moab, and all that are in the utmost corners, that dwell in the wilderness: *for all these nations are uncircumcised, and all the house of Israel are uncircumcised in the heart!*" Jer. ix, 25, 26.

It is equally evident that this was the case with the nation generally in the time of Moses, or it would never have been needful to rebuke and exhort them in such terms as these: "Circumcise therefore the foreskin of your heart, and be no more stiff-necked:" וּמַלְתֶּם אֵת עׇרְלַת לְבַבְכֶם וְעׇרְפְּכֶם לֹא תַקְשׁוּ עוֹד Deut. x, 16. And by referring to different passages of the historical and prophetical books, it would be very easy to point out many other periods in which the great mass of the nation were evidently strangers to that new heart and new spirit, of which we are speaking.

What has been so often, and so generally the case heretofore, may be so still, and at this present day. It is therefore, not at all improbable that *you, who are now reading this exhortation, are yet uncircumcised in the heart.*

And *if so,* what a mighty change must be wrought in your soul! and how seriously and earnestly should you seek after it. Oh that conviction it is, that I address you, in the words of your own prophets: vide Jer. xlii, 15, 16; Ezek. xviii, 30—32; and Jer. xvii, 13, 14.

My brethren, in conclusion, allow me to urge upon you, the necessity of diligent inquiry and earnest prayer. Vide Prov. ii, 1—6; iii, 5—8; and Eccl. ix, 10; xi, 3. We have already seen that David was very earnest in prayer for this *new heart*—and you cannot do better than adopt the earnest language of his soul, as you find it in the fifty-first, and in many other Psalms. And the Lord gives you a very important declaration on this point:— for in reference to those gracious promises of a new heart and a new spirit, which we have already quoted, he tells us expressly, "Thus saith the Lord God; I will yet for this be inquired of by the house of Israel, to do it for them." Ezek. xxxvi, 37. כֹּה אָמַר אֲדֹנָי יֱהֹוִה עוֹד זֹאת אִדָּרֵשׁ לְבֵית־יִשְׂרָאֵל לַעֲשׂוֹת לָהֶם אַרְבֶּה אֹתָם כַּצֹּאן אָדָם׃ Whence we learn, that waiting humbly upon God with earnest prayer, is his appointed way of obtaining this inestimable blessing. Begin therefore without delay. The precious moments which can never be recalled, are rapidly passing away. Eternity—Eternity is just at hand. And oh! who can tell what will be the miserable condition of your soul, if you should be swept into eternity unprepared!!!

I am well aware that the very circumstance of being your brother according to the flesh, will tend to strengthen your prejudices against this humble attempt to address you. I beseech you, let not this be your stumbling block; think not that I persuade you to embrace christianity because I have done the same; believe me, it is simply because I am convinced it is the religion of the Old Testament, and without it, you can have no hope of salvation. Think not that Jesus Christ came to destroy your religion, nay, he came to establish it. He has declared that "he came to seek the lost sheep of Israel; that salvation is of the Jews:" Matt. xv, 24; John iv, 22; Luke xix, 10. Is it your stumbling block that it is now also the religion of the Gentiles? Then do you stumble against your very scriptures, against the word of God, for they declare " that the Gentiles shall seek to the ensign which shall be set up unto the people, and that ensign was to be the root of Jesse, even the Messiah, the son of David, and that "the earth shall be full of the knowledge of the Lord, as the waters cover the sea." Isaiah xi, 10, 9. Nor am I insensible of the hasty and confident judgment which most of you perhaps will be apt to pass upon me. Perhaps you may say of me, He is a contemptible hypocrite; he is become a Christian for the sake of temporal advantages. Whatever you may venture to say, I pray that God may forgive you; and lead me by his Spirit to a just knowledge of myself, and of his holy will; for if, as you may imagine, I have embraced Christianity for the sake of worldly advantage, then am I indeed "of all men the most miserable," (1 Cor. xv, 19;) the most guilty: but if, as I have conscientiously stated, I have scriptural proofs, and above all, an evidence in my heart, that Jesus is indeed the Messiah the Son of the living God, the Lord both of Jews and gentiles, I cannot but cry out, with the Psalmist,—" Come and taste that the Lord is gracious!" Psalm xxxiv, 9. Come and see Him of whom Moses and the prophets have spoken, Jesus of Nazareth." John i, 39, 45; Acts xxvi, 22. "To the law and to the testimony;" (Isaiah viii, 20;) there seek the Lord Jesus Christ, and you will find him. He is not only the subject of the New Testament, but of the Old also; the New is but an accurate fulfilment of the Old. In conclusion, I would earnestly request you to peruse with attention, the contents of this little volume, as being small streams derived from a great fountain; and should you while reading it, meet with any thing not congenial with your sentiments or feelings, let me beseech you not to throw it aside in haste, but seriously reconsider the subject. May the God of Abraham, Isaac, and Jacob, bless the reading of it to your souls, and grant, that you and I, my dear brethren, may join our cheerful voices in singing, "Hosanna to the Son of David:" Matt. xxi. 9, 15. And may we all meet around his throne of glory to sing redeeming grace for ever. *Amen.*

To my Friends and Brethren in the Lord Jesus Christ.

IN the foregoing statement of the grounds of my profession of Christianity, and of my hope as a disciple of Christ, I have addressed myself to my brethren according to the flesh. These pages will fall into the hands of some whom I feel a pleasure in regarding as my friends, and brethren in Christ. To you, my Christian friends, especially in this City, I must briefly address myself, before closing this little volume. I wish to take the opportunity of assuring you of the deep sense I entertain of that kindness, which you have uniformly shewn me, and of respectfully urging you to continued and unwearied exertions on behalf of the lost sheep of the House of Israel. When from a conviction of my duty, to forsake all and to follow Christ, I formed the painful resolution of leaving a beloved father, brothers, sisters, and friends,—and vacating a situation in the Synagogue, which afforded a competency—it was to enter the wide world as an outcast, to encounter the unkind treatment of my Jewish brethren, and the suspicions of Christians. Many trials I have indeed endured since that time, which can be properly appreciated by those only who have passed through similar circumstances, and for conscience sake have made similar sacrifices. But, on these I must not, and will not dwell. I advert to them only for the purpose of rendering my acknowledgments to those who in the time of my need "remembered the words of our Lord Jesus, how he said, it is more blessed to give than to receive:" Acts xx, 35. Next to that peace of mind I have found in believing in Christ Jesus the Lord, and which I hope never to relinquish for all this world's honours and wealth, has been the consolation arising from the sympathy and kindness of my christian friends in every season of difficulty. They will accept my thanks for all the temporal assistance they have afforded me, but especially for the spiritual advice and encouragement by which I have been instructed and established in the "truth as it is in Jesus." Eph. iv. 21. It would be ingratitude of no ordinary kind were I not to acknowledge the obligations I owe to many esteemed friends among the Dissenters, as well as Episcopalians, though it is to the latter, as a Christian body, I have attached myself. I am anxious, my Christian friends, that you should do for others of my own people, what you have done for me. Perhaps some of my readers may have hitherto done nothing towards the conversion of the Jews; and others, it may be, have not exerted themselves so as to be able to say, "they have done what they could;" Mark xiv. 8. Suffer me then to remind you of some considerations which may serve to shew, that it is your duty and privilege to seek the salvation of *Jews* as well as Gentiles.

An appeal may be made to the *common feelings of humanity*, and especially to *the commiseration of Christian hearts.*

The state of the Jews is truly pitiable. That curse which their ancestors invoked, has had from age to age in their bitter experience a most tremendous accomplishment. They cried out not in vain before Pilate's bar, "his blood be on us and on our children;" Matt. xxvii, 25. Scattered through every country, the predictions of their prophets respecting them minutely fulfilled, they have, for many centuries, been a "byeword and a proverb;" (Deut. xxviii, 37,) the very scorn and outcast of the world. What persecutions, what massacres, what confiscations, what expulsion, and banishments, have not this miserable people endured in all ages of their dispersion. But if their *temporal* circumstances are wretched, how much more wretched is their *spiritual* condition? Many of them are not ashamed to profess that they think as little of Moses as of Christ, and found all their eternal hopes on the uncertainty of Deism. Their *morals* are as abandoned as their *principles*. For the most part they are given to the unbounded gratification of criminal passions; they even dare to justify them, and by the most awful of all deceptions, sin on principle, alleging on the authority of the Rabbies, that fornication is not forbidden by the law of Moses. Now, if neither " fornicators, nor adulterers, nor thieves, nor covetous, nor drunkards, nor extortioners, shall enter the kingdom of God,"

(1 Cor. vii. 9, 10.) can we imagine a state of more wretched and guilty ignorance, or one which makes a stronger appeal to the compassion of christians? It may, perhaps, be pleaded that there are other persons whose circumstances are equally pitiable, and who, from their more immediate connection with us, demand our preference. But cannot the Jew advance claims of gratitude and justice on the christian, far beyond any other class of men in the world? For, to whom do we owe *gratitude for past favours* in an equal degree? To whom were first " committed the oracles of God?" Rom. iii. 2.—*To the Jews*. Who preserved the truth which we now enjoy, preserved it from age to age, while the whole earth was full of darkness? *The Jews.*—Nay, christians, by whom have you been reconciled to God? Was he not a *Jew*, who shed his own blood, that by his death you might live; through whose intercession the Holy Ghost condescends to dwell in your heart, to cheer you by his presence in all your trials, and to support you by his grace in every time of need? Who was Peter, or John, or Paul, through whom we have received " the faith which is in Christ Jesus:" (2 Tim. iii, 15:) were they not all Jews? Yet they did not count their lives dear, if so be they " might preach the unsearchable riches of Christ among the

G

Gentiles:" Eph. iii; 8. And will you pass by the Israelites in careless indifference, when any attempt which may be made on their behalf requires not the relinquishment of one of your ordinary comforts? Far from you be such ingratitude. You have a *debt to pay* which cannot be withheld without the most flagrant dishonesty. It is true, that for their unrepented transgressions, God has "scattered them" over the whole earth (Deut. xxx, 3:) yet that affords no excuse to those who may have added to the afflictions of his people; it cannot justify any neglect of their best interests. It was an expression of Frederick, king of Prussia, a most determined enemy of all religions; "I have learned by the experience of ages, that no man ever touched that people but he smarted for it." A remark which the voice of inspiration as well as the experience of mankind has abundantly confirmed. God has declared by his prophets, that when he revisits his people, and takes away the veil from their hearts, he will judge and punish their oppressors. "Behold, at that time I will undo all that afflict thee, I will contend with him that contendeth with thee; I will feed them that oppress thee with their own flesh, and they shall be drunken with their own blood as with sweet wine; and all flesh shall know that I the Lord am thy Saviour and thy Redeemer.

Yea, they shall dwell with confidence in their own land, when I have executed judgment upon all those that despise them round about them." Zeph. iii, 19; Isa. xlix, 25, 26; Ezek. xxviii, 26. Have the nations, then, no reason to tremble? For where is that country which has not despised, afflicted, and contended with Israel?

National iniquity must be visited by national calamity, or the guilt of it be removed by national repentance. Whenever God shall visit our crimes, he will not forget the affliction of his ancient people, unless we repent and make a return of good to those whose forefathers have received so much evil at our hands. "Because thou hast had a perpetual hatred, and hast shed the blood of the children of Israel, by the force of the sword, in the time of their calamity, therefore as I live, saith the Lord God, I will prepare thee unto blood, and blood shall pursue thee, since thou hast not hated blood, even blood shall pursue thee:" Ezek. xxxv, 5, 6. There is no other way of averting this heavy judgment, than by testifying against the sin of our forefathers, and labouring to repair the evils they have committed. Can it be considered otherwise than an *imperious duty to attempt the conversion of the Jews?* If bowels of compassion form a peculiar feature in the christian character, if ingratitude be a monstrous sin, if it be our duty to be just in all our dealings, and whenever we have wronged others to make restitution to the utmost of our power, if to lessen sin, and to seek the prosperity of the nation, by advancing it in holiness, be the duty of a christian, then it is our duty to attend to the present state of the Jews, and to employ means for their conversion. Christ blamed the Jews for their neglect and contempt of the Gentiles. And are the Gentiles less reprehensible for their neglect and contempt of the Jews? Another class of motives may be drawn from *considerations of a more refined nature*, and which surely will not fail of their due influence on *the true believer*. Does the glory of God lie near your heart? We are taught to expect that his name will be sanctified in the most extraordinary degree, when he has "gathered his people from all countries whither I have scattered them:" Jer. xxiii. 3. 8. Is the honour of the Redeemer the subject of our daily prayer? What can add so great a lustre to his crown, as when all Israel shall bow to his dominion? Do you feel compassion for the souls of sinners? None need greater compassion than the Jews. Do you desire the conversion of the heathen? This great and glorious object will never be fully obtained, till all Israel shall come in; " For if the fall of them be the riches of the world, and the diminishing of them be the riches of the Gentiles, how much more their fulness? If the casting away of them be the reconciling of the world, what shall the recovery of them be, but life from the dead:" Rom. xi, 14, 15. The high honour of evangelizing the world, and introducing that glorious period, " when the earth shall be covered with the knowledge of the Lord, as the waters cover the sea," (Isa. xi, 9,) seems to be reserved, in the divine counsel, for that favoured nation, "in whom all the families of the earth ever have been and ever shall be blessed:" Gen. xii, 3. The Jews are every where dispersed, they are trained up in the knowledge of the languages, habits, and manners, of the nations amongst whom they dwell, and are thereby prepared to rank among the best qualified and most useful missionaries, whenever " the Lord shall take the veil from their hearts:" 2 Cor. iii, 15. O for that great and glorious day, when Israel " shall look upon Him whom they have pierced;" (Zech. xii, 10;) when we shall behold with wonder and astonishment, that that spirit of prophecy, which, commencing as early as the fall of Adam, has pervaded all times; and extending itself to the final consummation of all things, has been fulfilled with peculiar exactness, in every important event that befel the church, even from its first establishment, down to that awful period of expectation, when the great plan of divine grace shall be brought to a glorious conclusion, and the mysterious counsels of the Almighty respecting it, shall be for ever closed in judgment.

The peculiar complexion of the times affords great encouragement to attempt the conversion of the Jews, at the present period.

There can be no doubt with those who believe the Scriptures, that a period is marked out in the counsels of God, for the conversion of the Jews. " I would not, brethren, that ye should be ignorant of this mystery, lest ye be wise in your own conceits, that blindness in part has happened to Israel, until the fulness of the Gentiles be come in;" till the time be completed for the exclusive enjoyment of Christian privileges by the Gentile world; "and so all Israel shall be saved," the whole nation shall be converted, " as it is written, There shall come out of Zion the Deliverer, and shall turn away ungodliness from Jacob:" Rom. xi. 25, 26, &c.

Shall we not mark the signs of the times? Ought not the voice of God, in his providential interpositions, to be regarded?

The immediate design of our Lord's own ministry, was to call the Jews; and therefore, in our attempts to convert them, we are particularly treading in his steps. His last command to his apostles was, "that they should preach the gospel to every creature," not excepting *any* sinner of *any* nation: yet forgiveness of sins through his name was " first to be preached at Jerusalem:" Luke xxiv, 47.

It was unbelief at first, and it is unbelief now, which alone excludes them from the blessings of His kingdom: vide Rom. xi, 23. Allowing, therefore, that no *national* conversion of the Jews can be expected before the destined period; or even that there is no reason to believe that period near at hand, why should we content ourselves with attempting the conversion of all other sinners except the Jews? Some of them may be saved, though not all; for, however distant that period of their *national restoration* may be, God has no where forbidden the expectation of individual conversion. My Christian brethren, may I not ask *you* what *you* have done, in behalf of the conversion of the Jews? Have you been as much interested for the Jew, as you have for the heathen? Have you had your prayer-meetings for the conversion of the Jew? Can you say with the apostle Paul,—" Brethren, my heart's desire and prayer to God for Israel is, that they may be saved?" If you really have done this,—if you have prayed that God would pour out the Spirit of grace and supplication on the House of Israel,—if you have exerted yourselves according to your ability in behalf of that good and glorious cause, remember what God said to Abram, " I will bless them that bless thee:" Gen. xii, 3. And if you have not done this, let me intreat you to begin now. Remember the poor Israelite has an immortal soul, as well as the heathen. And shall you give to *one and not to another?* Surely, when the Christian takes the blessed book of God into his hands, and reads the sixty-second chapter of Isaiah, he cannot say that he will not attempt any thing in behalf of the Jew. Pray, my brethren, for the lost sheep of the House of Israel whenever you pray for yourselves. Think of the dangers, the temptations, the difficulties to which Jews are exposed, and remember the efficacy of believing prayer. " Now unto him that is able to keep us from falling, and to present us faultless before the presence of his glory with exceeding joy, to the only wise God our Saviour, be glory and majesty, dominion and power, both now and ever." *Amen.*

Printed by S. Wilkin, Upper Haymarket, Norwich.
Jan. 1st, 1830.

www.ingramcontent.com/pod-product-compliance
Lightning Source LLC
Chambersburg PA
CBHW070001210725
29880CB00010B/875